MW01474451

The Legal Stuff

My EPIC Toddler Journal by Rachael Cartmell. Published by Nurtured Me Ltd.

Copyright © 2018 Rachael Cartmell. All rights reserved.

No part of this publication may be reproduced, stored, or transmitted in any form or by any means, electronic, mechanical, photocopying, recording, scanning, or otherwise, without the prior written permission of the author. Requests to the author and publisher for permission should be addressed to:

hello@myepicjournals.com

Limitation of liability/disclaimer of warranty: While the publisher and author have used their best efforts in preparing this journal, they make no representations or warranties with respect to the accuracy or completeness of the contents of this document and specifically disclaim any implied warranties of merchantability or fitness for particular purpose. No warranty may be created or extended by sales representatives, promoters, or written sales materials.

The advice and strategies contained herein may not be suitable for your situation. You should consult with a professional where appropriate. Neither the publisher nor author shall be liable for any loss or any other damages, including but not limited to special, incidental, consequential, or other damages.

Due to the dynamic nature of the Internet, certain links and website information contained in this publication may have changed. The author and publisher make no representations to the current accuracy of the web information shared.

ISBN: 9-781790-158386

My Epic Toddler Journal

OF Lochlan + Mama

For H and A
For your unending love and fascination with the world, and for being the
inspiration for creating this journal.

Thank you to:
T and J, for being such amazing role models and inspiring me to do more.

H, C and S, for believing in me.

P, for your unending patience and for keeping me going with putting this out there into the world.

M, for lots of last minute things.

Contents

Introduction	6
Routines	7
How to Use this Journal	8
About Me	9
Farm Animals	19
Rainbow Colours	65
Our World	111
Notes	158

Welcome to your My EPIC Toddler Journal

Are you one of those people who say how much they are going to write down all those amazing things their child does or says? Well this is the book that will help keep you accountable to doing that.

Not only do you have a page per day to keep notes on all the lovely things that happen, that you're going to want to remember when your adorable toddlers are teenagers and don't talk to you anymore, but there is also space for them to join in with the journal, be a part of their own journey, create their own epic and learn to reflect on their day with you. I hope that completing this journal together each day will become a much treasured part of your day.

You'll be able to see their drawings/doodles/scribbling progress throughout the journal. As well as lots of extra bonus guided journal pages such as their favourite things, growth charts, favourite foods and who they want to be when they're big. Finally, there are activity pages which link to www.myepicjournals.com, providing even more activities, recipes, experiments and fun to do together.

On the next few pages, you'll find out more about how to use the My Epic Toddler Journal to the full, in a way that isn't overwhelming. As you complete the journal together, and build on it with further journals, it will leave you with an incredible account of your children's childhood and help to build an extra special bond between you.

About the Author

Rachael Cartmell is a mother to 2 girls. After waiting for 9 years for her first to arrive, her second came just 16 months later. She needed to create a bedtime routine to fit both of her children together and found talking and writing about their day fit in really well. She is an advocate of natural parenting, mama time and learning through play, and can usually be found out exploring with her children or in her digital home at www.Nurtured.me

Routines

I have found routines to be so important in maximising our time. When I first became a Mother, there was so much advice around on routines, and the importance of establishing them with a newborn, and as my babies grew, those routines developed with us. When my second was born, I had to start from scratch and create a whole new routine that worked for a 16 month old and a newborn together, and I couldn't find anything that suited us in any of the books that I read that claimed to have THE answer.

I found something that worked for us though, and it came about through being free for a few weeks, seeing how things naturally flowed, and then trying to fit a routine around what we needed in our day, to try to help speed things up a little.

When I became a single parent, we had to change our routines again, as now it was just me doing everything with our girls, and we had to learn to work together. Throughout my time as a Mother, the times that have been the most fun, the most free and the most relaxed are the times that our routine has been sorted. Without it our life just descends into a chaos of waiting around, getting stressed from nagging and even arguments between my children.

Our bedtime routine is the most established of our routines, and we love it. My children, even though they are still so small actually ask to go to bed as they love our routine so much. You can read more about it over at www.nurtured.me/routines.

We have done a form of journalling since the very beginning, but I felt I wanted to create something beautiful, that could be used by other families in their routines too. Hence My Epic Toddler Journal was born. Used as part of a bedtime routine, it really does wrap up the day so nicely, and leaves no space for anything other than restful sleep. Talking through the day with your children is such a lovely practice, even from the time before they can join in the conversation. It allows time to reflect on the day, new discoveries, favourite things, funny moments and of course, memory worthy events.

By making notes with them, allowing your children to join in with what you write about and providing them space to make their own marks on the day as well this journal will become a much loved part of your everyday.

How to use this Journal

Each evening, as part of your bedtime routine, take a few minutes to snuggle up with your child and fill in the daily sheet.

As you come across a special page, fill that in too. If you don't have anything to write on a particular day, just let your little one take over the whole page with their crayons. You can complete the About Me section at any stage, or on different days. The pages here are activities in themselves.

Try not to feel overwhelmed with the journal, just take it one day at a time, and you will soon come to see it as a lovely event in itself. Your toddler will love some one to one time with you. We cherish our journalling time together, and as my children grow, I have found it a great place to 'check-in' with them about how they're feeling.

Now head to www.myepicjournals.com to find out more about ways to use this journal and access the bonus features.

about ME

Snapshot of now:

My name is: Lochlan

My age is: 2

My hair is: brown

How big am I? ballerinas tutu

My personality is: ever changing

We live: Manlius

Our neighbours are: Jenny + Lucas, Rebeka + Reno

Date: 1-7-20

ME:

People I see most often are:

Name	Relationship	What I call them
		Nana + PJ
		Kuma
		Bop Bep + mimi
		Grandma

My usual routines:

Weekday:

Weekend:

Trace around your hand and foot

Date: _____

My Epic Toddler Journal

Ask your child these questions, without prompting, and write down their answers, whatever they are. These are so lovely to look back on as they grow.

What is your name?	Lochlan
What is your favourite colour?	orange
When is your birthday?	I forgot
How old are you?	2 years
How old am I?	8
What is your favourite song?	Take me home tonight
What is your favourite animal?	lions
What do you like to eat?	Carrots + Strawberries
Who is your best friend?	Aubry ?
What makes you happy?	music
What are you scared of?	winnie the pooh
Where is your favourite place to go?	Target
What do you want to be when you grow up?	a girl + drink beer
What is your favourite toy?	grocery shop
Where does money come from?	bank
Where do you live?	at home

Memory is a way of holding onto the things you love, the things you have, and the things you never want to lose!

Who is around me:

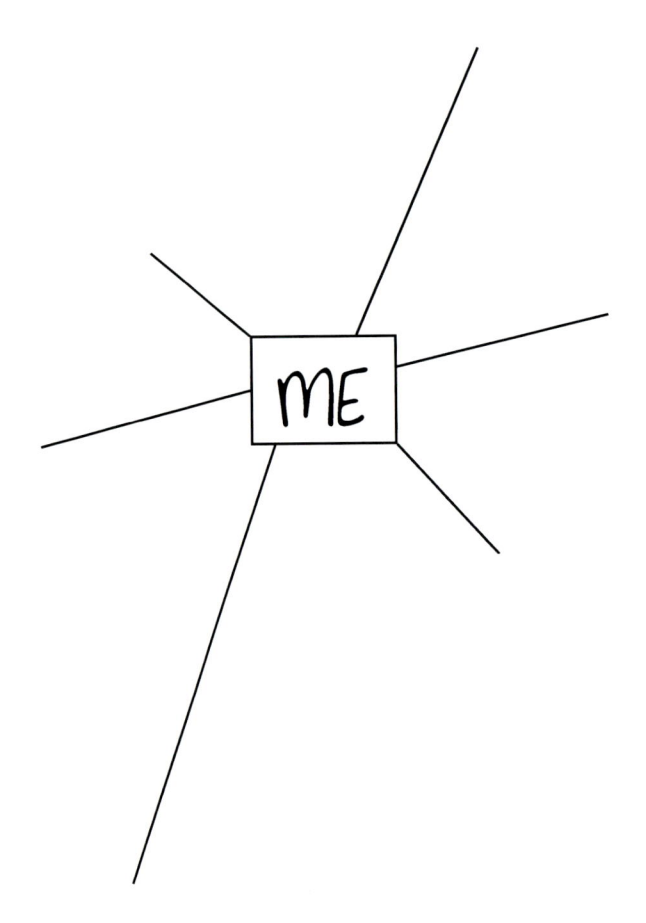

| ME |

Stick in photo's, draw pictures or write names

Who do you love?   Who loves you?

What does love feel like inside you?

My Epic Toddler Journal

The BEST things in life are not things

My Bedtime Routine is... Date: _____

My Favourite Toys...   Date: _____

My Favourite Books...

FARM ANIMALS

Weather: ☀️ ☁️🌤 🌈 🌧 💨 ❄️ Date: 12·26·19 M T W T̃ F S S

What we did today:

"We went to the manlius library"... no we didn't
we played with new Christmas toys and went to dinner at Texas Roadhouse. Our favorite xmas toy above all else is a $16.00 flashlight.

Our favourite books today:

The Pout Pout fish

My today...

Something I am grateful for today:

Today I felt:

Weather: ☀️ ☁️ 🌈 🌧️ 💨 ❄️   Date: M T W T F S S

What we did today:

Our favourite books today:

Today I loved...

Something I am grateful for today:

Today I felt: 😀 🙂 😍 😛 😆 😌 😟 😣 🙁 😠

My Epic Toddler Journal

Weather: ☀ ☁ 🌈 🌧 💨 ❄   Date: M T W T F S S

What we did today:

Our favourite books today:

What I remember about today...

Something I am grateful for today:

Today I felt: 😀 🙂 😍 😋 😆 😌 🤔 😖 😟 😠

22

My Epic Toddler Journal

ANIMAL BISCUITS

INGREDIENTS

175g	Margarine/Butter
3 tbs	Honey
2	Eggs
250g	Flour

METHOD

1. Preheat oven to 180 °C (350 °F).

2. In a large bowl, weigh 175g margarine and add 3tbs honey. Mix well, using a mixer if you have one, or a wooden spoon and lots of arm power if not.

3. Add 2 eggs and 150g of the flour and mix again the same way until combined.

4. Add the remaining 100g flour, and fold in using a wooden spoon to combine into the thick dough.

   (It may need a splash of milk, it may need a little more flour, depending on the consistency and your flour.)

5. Wrap the dough in film and place in fridge for up to an hour, or freezer for 10-15 minutes to rest.

6. Roll onto a floured surface and have fun cutting out your shapes. You can form a ball and re-roll to press out more shapes.

7. Place onto a floured baking tray/sheet and bake for around 10 minutes.

8. Allow to cool, then devour, safe in the knowledge they are free of refined sugar free.

visit myepicjournals.com for more activities

Photo's of Me Making.......

Weather: ☀️ ☁️ 🌈 🌧️ 💨 ❄️   Date: M T W T F S S

What we did today:

Our favourite books today:

Today we did this...

Something I am grateful for today:

Today I felt: 😄 🙂 😍 😛 😆 😌 😟 😕 ☹️ 😠

My Epic Toddler Journal

25

Weather: ☀️ ☁️ 🌈 🌧️ 💨 ❄️   Date: M T W T F S S

What we did today:

Our favourite books today:

I saw this today...

Something I am grateful for today:

Today I felt: 😀 🙂 😍 😜 😆 ☺️ 😟 😣 😦 😠

best DAY EVER

COLOUR ME

My Epic Toddler Journal

Weather: ☀ ☁ 🌈 🌧 💨 ❄ Date: M T W T F S S

What we did today:

Our favourite books today:

Today we...

Something I am grateful for today:

Today I felt: 😀 🙂 😍 😜 😆 😌 😐 😖 ☹ 😠

Weather: ☀️ ☁️ 🌈 🌧️ 💨 ❄️   Date: M T W T F S S

What we did today:

Our favourite books today:

Today I felt…

Something I am grateful for today:

Today I felt: 😀 🙂 😍 😜 😆 😌 😟 😧 😕 😠

My Epic Toddler Journal

Weekly Check In:

This week, for the first time I...:

My favourite meals this week:

Books I've read this week:

Favourite Toys to play with this week:

My favourite thing this week:

I made someone most proud when:

Weather: Date: M T W T F S S

Our favourite books today:

My today...

Today I felt:

Find 10 Differences

Weather: ☀️ ☁️ 🌈 🌧️ 💨 ❄️   Date: M T W T F S S

What we did today:

Our favourite books today:

Today I loved...

Something I am grateful for today:

Today I felt: 😀 🙂 😍 😋 😆 😊 😟 😖 😞 😠

My Epic Toddler Journal

33

Weather: ☀ ☁ 🌈 🌧 💨 ❄ Date: M T W T F S S

What we did today:

Our favourite books today:

What I remember about today...

Something I am grateful for today:

Today I felt: 😀 🙂 😍 😋 😆 😌 😟 😕 ☹ 😠

34 *My Epic Toddler Journal*

Weather: ☀️ ☁️ 🌈 🌧️ 💨 ❄️   Date: M T W T F S S

What we did today:

Our favourite books today:

Today we did this...

Something I am grateful for today:

Today I felt: 😀 🙂 😍 😛 😆 😌 😕 😖 🙁 😠

My Epic Toddler Journal

I can draw a sheep   Date:_____

Weather: ☀ ☁ 🌈 🌧 💨 ❄   Date: M T W T F S S

What we did today:

Our favourite books today:

I saw this today...

Something I am grateful for today:

Today I felt: 😀 🙂 😍 😜 😆 😌 🤔 😟 ☹ 😠

My Epic Toddler Journal

Weather: ☀ ☁ 🌈 🌧 💨 ❄ Date: M T W T F S S

What we did today:

Our favourite books today:

Today we...

Something I am grateful for today:

Today I felt: 😃 🙂 😍 😜 😆 😌 🤔 😟 😕 😠

Weather: ☀ ☁ 🌈 🌧 💨 ❄   Date: M T W T F S S

What we did today:

Our favourite books today:

Today I felt...

Something I am grateful for today:

Today I felt: 😀 🙂 😍 😋 😆 😌 😟 😣 ☹ 😠

My Epic Toddler Journal   *39*

Weekly Check In:

This week, for the first time I...:

My favourite meals this week:

Books I've read this week:

Favourite Toys to play with this week:

My favourite thing this week:

I made someone most proud when:

Pictures of me with animals

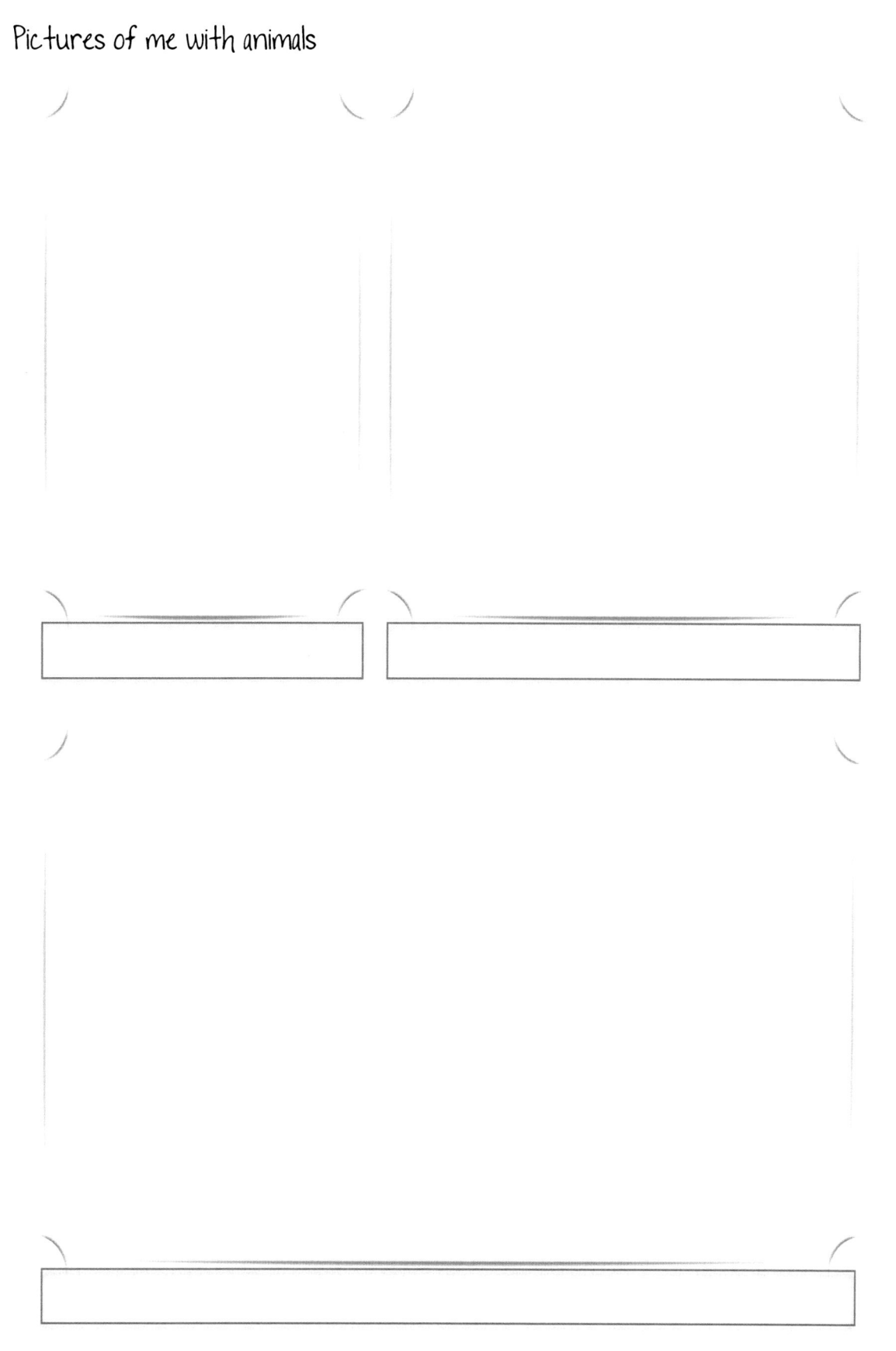

Weather: ☀ ☁ 🌈 🌧 💨 ❄   Date: M T W T F S S

What we did today:

Our favourite books today:

My today...

Something I am grateful for today:

Today I felt:

My Epic Toddler Journal

Weather: ☀ ☁ 🌈 🌧 💨 ❄   Date: M T W T F S S

What we did today:

Our favourite books today:

Today I loved...

Something I am grateful for today:

Today I felt: 😁 🙂 😍 😛 😆 😌 🤔 😟 ☹ 😠

My Epic Toddler Journal   43

Weather: ☀ ☁ 🌈 🌧 💨 ❄ Date: M T W T F S S

What we did today:

Our favourite books today:

What I remember about today…

Something I am grateful for today:

Today I felt: 😃 🙂 😍 😜 😆 ☺ 😟 😖 😣 😠

My Epic Toddler Journal

I AM A HERO

Weather: ☀ ☁ 🌈 🌧 💨 ❄ Date: M T W T F S S

What we did today:

Our favourite books today:

Today we did this...

Something I am grateful for today:

Today I felt: 😃 🙂 😍 😛 😆 😌 🤨 😕 ☹️ 😠

46

My Epic Toddler Journal

Weather: ☀️ ☁️ 🌈 🌧️ 💨 ❄️   Date: M T W T F S S

What we did today:

Our favourite books today:

I saw this today...

Something I am grateful for today:

Today I felt: 😀 🙂 😍 😛 😆 😌 😟 😣 ☹️ 😠

My Epic Toddler Journal   47

FARM ANIMAL SEARCH

Go to a farm and tick the boxes or fill in how many you can count when you see the animal.

Weather: ☀ ☁ 🌈 🌧 💨 ❄ Date: M T W T F S S

What we did today:

Our favourite books today:

Today we...

Something I am grateful for today:

Today I felt: 😀 🙂 😍 😋 😆 😌 🤔 😖 🙁 😠

My Epic Toddler Journal   49

Weather: ☀️ ☁️ 🌈 🌧️ 💨 ❄️   Date: M T W T F S S

What we did today:

Our favourite books today:

Today I felt...

Something I am grateful for today:

Today I felt: 😀 🙂 😍 😜 😆 😌 😟 😨 🙁 😠

Weekly Check In:

This week, for the first time I...:

My favourite meals this week:

Books I've read this week:

Favourite Toys to play with this week:

My favourite thing this week:

I made someone most proud when:

Weather: ☀ ☁ 🌈 🌧 💨 ❄ Date: M T W T F S S

What we did today:

Our favourite books today:

My today...

Something I am grateful for today:

Today I felt: 😀 🙂 😍 😜 😆 😌 😟 😖 ☹ 😠

Pictures of my favourite things

Weather: ☀ ☁ 🌈 🌧 💨 ❄   Date: MTWTFSS

What we did today:

Our favourite books today:

Today I loved...

Something I am grateful for today:

Today I felt: 😀 🙂 😍 😜 😆 😌 🤢 😟 ☹ 😠

Weather: ☀ ☁ 🌈 🌧 💨 ❄   Date: M T W T F S S

What we did today:

Our favourite books today:

What I remember about today...

Something I am grateful for today:

Today I felt: 😀 🙂 😍 😋 😆 😌 😕 😖 ☹ 😠

My Epic Toddler Journal

Weather: ☀️ ☁️ 🌈 🌧️ 💨 ❄️   Date: M T W T F S S

What we did today:

Our favourite books today:

Today we did this...

Something I am grateful for today:

Today I felt: 😀 🙂 😍 😛 😆 😌 😟 😣 ☹️ 😠

FARM ANIMAL SILHOUETTE

Help the animals with their shadows

Weather: ☀️ ☁️ 🌈 🌧️ 💨 ❄️   Date: M T W T F S S

What we did today:

Our favourite books today:

I saw this today...

Something I am grateful for today:

Today I felt: 😃 🙂 😍 😜 😆 😌 😟 😕 😠

58

My Epic Toddler Journal

Weather: ☀️ ☁️ 🌈 🌧️ 💨 ❄️   Date: M T W T F S S

What we did today:

Our favourite books today:

Today we...

Something I am grateful for today:

Today I felt: 😀 🙂 😍 😛 😆 😌 🤔 😖 🙁 😠

My Epic Toddler Journal

Weather: ☀ ☁ 🌈 🌧 💨 ❄   Date: M T W T F S S

What we did today:

Our favourite books today:

Today I felt...

Something I am grateful for today:

Today I felt: 😀 🙂 😍 😛 😆 😌 😟 😕 ☹ 😠

60

My Epic Toddler Journal

Weekly Check In:

This week, for the first time I...:

My favourite meals this week:

Books I've read this week:

Favourite Toys to play with this week:

My favourite thing this week:

I made someone most proud when:

Pictures of me

Reflection Page

Use this space to write a note to your little one this month. Did you go anywhere new that they enjoyed? Did they do something to make you proud? Did they do something kind? Did they make you laugh? Maybe share how much you love them. Tell them a story, or write down a story they told you.

let me love you
a little more
before you're not
little any more

Rainbow Colours

Weather: ☀ ☁ 🌈 🌧 💨 ❄   Date: M T W T F S S

What we did today:

Our favourite books today:

My today...

Something I am grateful for today:

Today I felt: 😀 🙂 😍 😛 😆 😌 😟 😖 😕 😠

Weather: ☀ ☁ 🌈 🌧 💨 ❄   Date: M T W T F S S

What we did today:

Our favourite books today:

Today I loved...

Something I am grateful for today:

Today I felt: 😀 🙂 😍 😜 😆 😊 🤢 😟 🙁 😣

My Epic Toddler Journal

67

Weather: ☀ ☁ 🌈 🌧 💨 ❄   Date: M T W T F S S

What we did today:

Our favourite books today:

What I remember about today...

Something I am grateful for today:

Today I felt: 😀 🙂 😍 😜 😆 😌 😕 😣 😟 😠

When it rains LOOK FOR RAINBOWS When it's dark LOOK FOR STARS

Weather: ☀ ☁ 🌈 🌧 💨 ❄ Date: M T W T F S S

What we did today:

Our favourite books today:

Today we did this...

Something I am grateful for today:

Today I felt: 😃 🙂 😍 😜 😆 😌 😕 😣 ☹ 😠

70

My Epic Toddler Journal

Weather: ☀ ☁ 🌈 🌧 💨 ❄   Date: M T W T F S S

What we did today:

Our favourite books today:

I saw this today...

Something I am grateful for today:

Today I felt: 😃 🙂 😍 😛 😆 😌 😕 😖 ☹ 😠

My Epic Toddler Journal

RAINBOW COLOURS

Can you find things to match these colours?

RED

BLUE

ORANGE

INDIGO

YELLOW

VIOLET

GREEN

Weather: ☀️ ☁️ 🌈 🌧️ 💨 ❄️   Date: M T W T F S S

What we did today:

Our favourite books today:

Today we...

Something I am grateful for today:

Today I felt: 😀 🙂 😍 😋 😆 😊 🤔 😖 ☹️ 😠

My Epic Toddler Journal

73

Weather: ☀ ☁ 🌈 🌧 💨 ❄ Date: M T W T F S S

What we did today:

Our favourite books today:

Today I felt...

Something I am grateful for today:

Today I felt: 😃 🙂 😍 😜 😆 😌 😟 😖 🙁 😠

Pictures of me wearing my favourite colours

Weekly Check In:

This week, for the first time I...:

My favourite meals this week:

Books I've read this week:

Favourite Toys to play with this week:

My favourite thing this week:

I made someone most proud when:

Weather: ☀️ ☁️ 🌈 🌧️ 💨 ❄️   Date: M T W T F S S

Our favourite books today:

My today...

Today I felt: 😃 🙂 😍 😛 😆 😊 🤢 😟 ☹️ 😠

My Epic Toddler Journal

77

Weather: ☀ ☁ 🌈 🌧 💨 ❄ Date: M T W T F S S

What we did today:

Our favourite books today:

Today I loved...

Something I am grateful for today:

Today I felt: 😀 🙂 😍 😋 😆 😌 😟 😖 😣 😠

Weather: ☀ ☁ 🌈 🌧 💨 ❄ Date: M T W T F S S

What we did today:

Our favourite books today:

What I remember about today...

Something I am grateful for today:

Today I felt: 😃 🙂 😍 😛 😆 😌 🤔 😟 🙁 😠

My Epic Toddler Journal

79

Be a rainbow in someone else's cloud

Weather: ☀ ☁ 🌈 🌧 💨 ❄ Date: M T W T F S S

What we did today:

Our favourite books today:

Today we did this...

Something I am grateful for today:

Today I felt: 😃 🙂 😍 😜 😆 😌 😟 😖 ☹ 😠

My Epic Toddler Journal

81

Weather: ☀ ☁ 🌈 🌧 💨 ❄ Date: M T W T F S S

What we did today:

Our favourite books today:

I saw this today...

Something I am grateful for today:

Today I felt: 😀 🙂 😍 😋 😆 😊 😕 😟 ☹ 😠

Pictures of me helping ......

Weather: Date: M T W T F S S

What we did today:

Our favourite books today:

Today we...

Something I am grateful for today:

Today I felt:

84

My Epic Toddler Journal

Weather: ☀ ☁ 🌈 🌧 💨 ❄ Date: M T W T F S S

What we did today:

Our favourite books today:

Today I felt...

Something I am grateful for today:

Today I felt: 😀 🙂 😍 😜 😆 😌 🤢 😖 🙁 😣

My Epic Toddler Journal

Weekly Check In:

This week, for the first time I...:

My favourite meals this week:

Books I've read this week:

Favourite Toys to play with this week:

My favourite thing this week:

I made someone most proud when:

Weather: ☀️ ☁️ 🌈 🌧️ 💨 ❄️   Date: M T W T F S S

Our favourite books today:

My today...

Today I felt: 😀 🙂 😍 😋 😆 😌 🤔 😖 🙁 😠

My Epic Toddler Journal   87

Weather: ☀ ☁ 🌈 🌧 💨 ❄   Date: M T W T F S S

What we did today:

Our favourite books today:

Today I loved...

Something I am grateful for today:

Today I felt: 😃 🙂 😍 😜 😆 😌 😕 😖 ☹ 😠

Pictures of my art

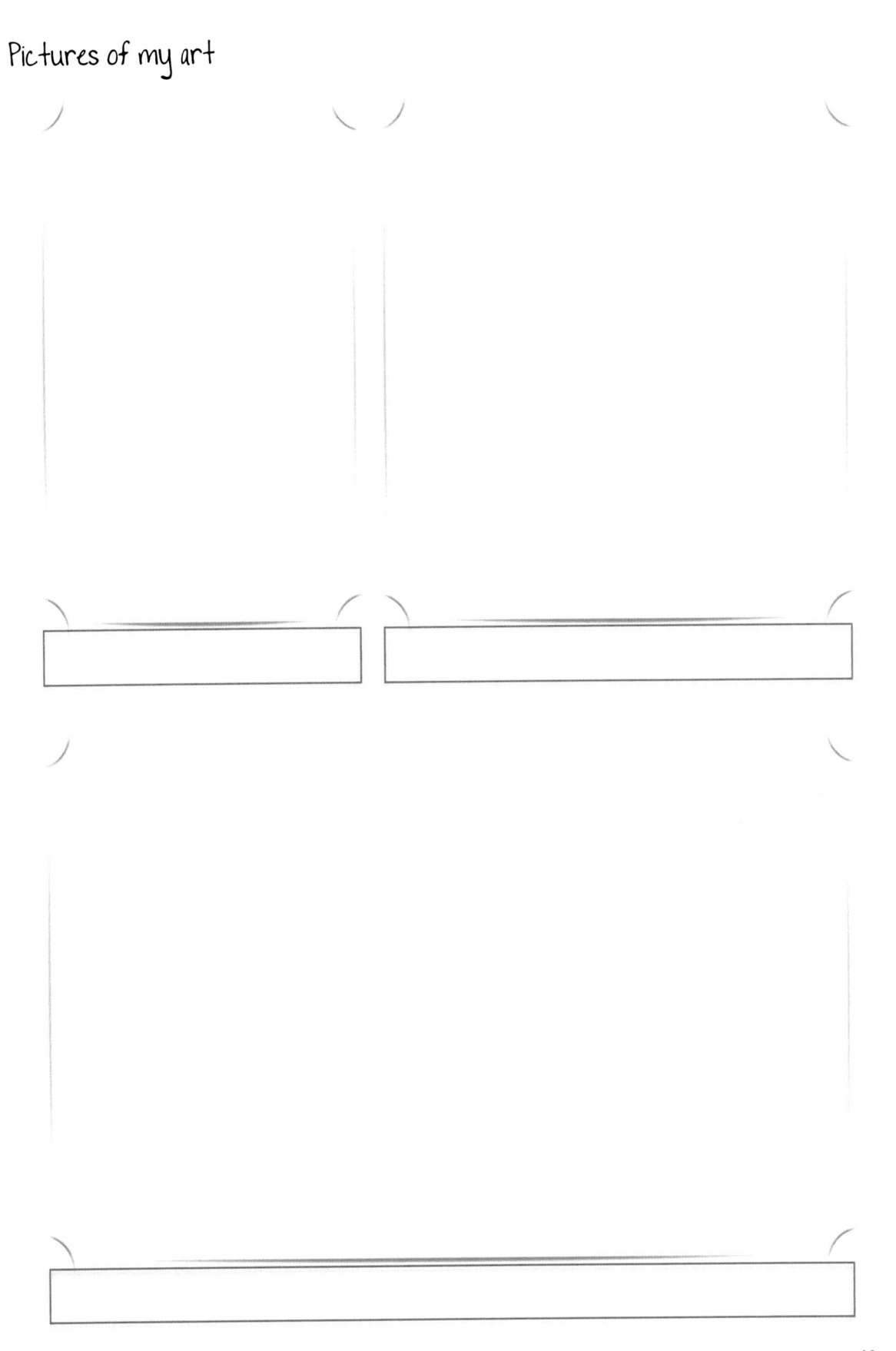

Weather: Date: M T W T F S S

What we did today:

Our favourite books today:

What I remember about today...

Something I am grateful for today:

Today I felt:

FINGERPRINT TREE

Use paints or stamp pads to fill the tree with your fingerprints

Weather: ☀️ ☁️ 🌈 🌧️ 💨 ❄️   Date: M T W T F S S

What we did today:

Our favourite books today:

Today we did this...

Something I am grateful for today:

Today I felt: 😀 🙂 😍 😜 😆 😌 🤔 😟 😖 😠

92

My Epic Toddler Journal

Weather: ☀ ☁ 🌈 🌧 💨 ❄   Date: M T W T F S S

What we did today:

Our favourite books today:

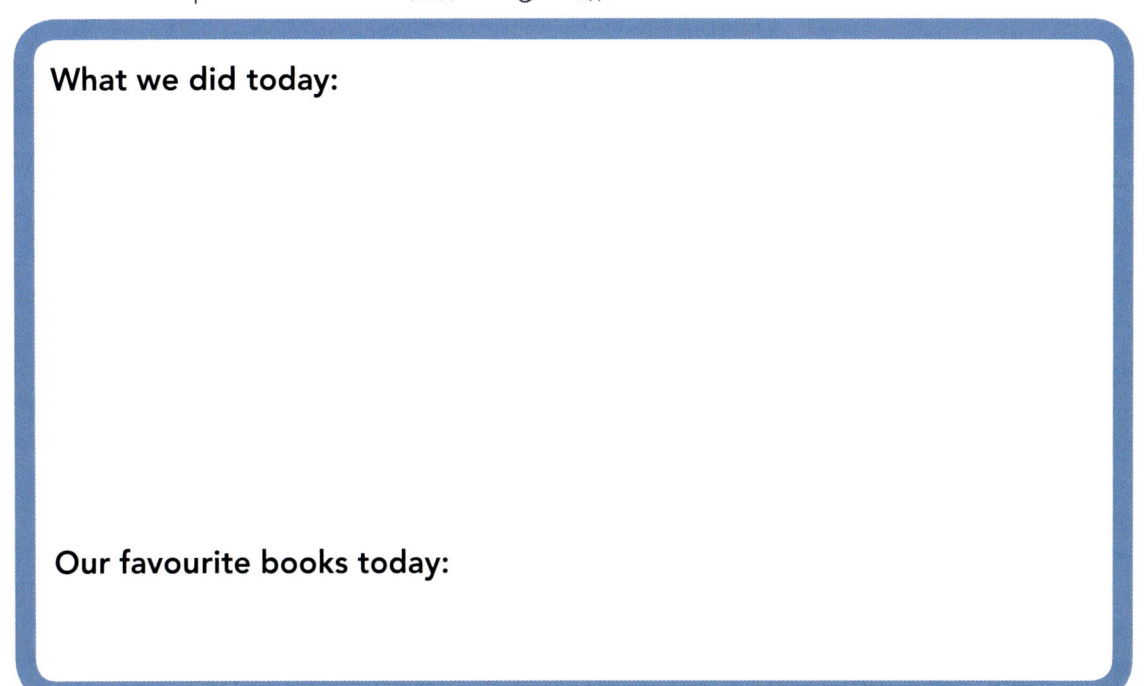

I saw this today...

Something I am grateful for today:

Today I felt: 😀 🙂 😍 😜 😆 😊 🤢 😰 🙁 😣

My Epic Toddler Journal   93

Weather: ☀ ☁ 🌈 🌧 💨 ❄ Date: M T W T F S S

What we did today:

Our favourite books today:

Today I felt...

Something I am grateful for today:

Today I felt: 😀 🙂 😍 😛 😄 😊 🤔 😖 ☹ 😠

My Epic Toddler Journal

Weather: Date: M T W T F S S

What we did today:

Our favourite books today:

Today we...

Something I am grateful for today:

Today I felt:

My Epic Toddler Journal

95

Rainbow Kebabs

Ingredients

Rainbow coloured fruits
Kebab sticks
optional - Fresh yogurt to dip

Method

1. Select fruits to cover each rainbow colour.

2. Cut the larger fruits to a similar size, I usually go by the size of the berries I've chosen, be it raspberries or strawberries. Blueberries can be added in multiples.

3. Skewer the fruit in the right order with the kebab sticks. Older children who won't poke their eyes, or their siblings can help with this task. Younger children can tell you which to skewer next to learn the rainbow.

4. Serve with yoghurt to dip the fruit into.

H&S Tip: Please be careful of any sharp points on your kebab sticks.

Weekly Check In:

This week, for the first time I...:

My favourite meals this week:

Books I've read this week:

Favourite Toys to play with this week:

My favourite thing this week:

I made someone most proud when:

Weather: ☀️ ☁️ 🌈 🌧️ 💨 ❄️   Date: M T W T F S S

What we did today:

Our favourite books today:

My today...

Something I am grateful for today:

Today I felt: 😀 🙂 😍 😜 😄 😌 🤔 😟 🙁 😠

I can draw with my favourite colours   Date: _____

Weather: ☀ ☁ 🌈 🌧 💨 ❄   Date: M T W T F S S

What we did today:

Our favourite books today:

Today I loved...

Something I am grateful for today:

Today I felt: 😀 🙂 😍 😜 😆 😌 🤔 😟 🙁 😠

Weather: ☀️ ☁️ 🌈 🌧️ 💨 ❄️   Date: M T W T F S S

What we did today:

Our favourite books today:

What I remember about today...

Something I am grateful for today:

Today I felt: 😃 🙂 🥰 😋 😆 😌 🤔 😟 😕 😠

My Epic Toddler Journal

101

EVERY CHILD IS AN ARTIST

~ PICASSO

EVERY CHILD IS AN ARTIST

Weather: ☀ ☁ 🌈 🌧 💨 ❄ Date: M T W T F S S

What we did today:

Our favourite books today:

Today we did this...

Something I am grateful for today:

Today I felt: 😀 🙂 😍 😜 😆 😌 🤢 😟 ☹ 😠

Weather: ☀ ☁ 🌈 🌧 💨 ❄   Date: M T W T F S S

What we did today:

Our favourite books today:

I saw this today...

Something I am grateful for today:

Today I felt: 😀 🙂 😍 😜 😆 😌 🤔 😖 ☹ 😠

My Epic Toddler Journal 105

My favourite pictures

Weather: ☀ ☁ 🌈 🌧 💨 ❄   Date: M T W T F S S

What we did today:

Our favourite books today:

Today we...

Something I am grateful for today:

Today I felt: 😃 🙂 😍 😛 😆 😌 😟 😣 🙁 😠

Weather: Date: M T W T F S S

What we did today:

Our favourite books today:

Today I felt...

Something I am grateful for today:

Today I felt:

Weekly Check In:

This week, for the first time I...:

My favourite meals this week:

Books I've read this week:

Favourite Toys to play with this week:

My favourite thing this week:

I made someone most proud when:

Reflection Page

Use this space to write a note to your little one this month. Did you go anywhere new that they enjoyed? Did they do something to make you proud? Did they do something kind? Did they make you laugh? Maybe share how much you love them. Tell them a story, or write down a story they told you.

OUR WORLD

IF MANY LITTLE PEOPLE IN MANY LITTLE PLACES DO MANY LITTLE THINGS THEY CAN CHANGE THE FACE OF THE EARTH

Weather: ☀ ☁ 🌈 🌧 💨 ❄   Date: M T W T F S S

Our favourite books today:

My today...

Today I felt: 😃 🙂 😍 😛 😆 😌 😟 😰 ☹ 😠

My Epic Toddler Journal   113

Weather: ☀ ☁ 🌈 🌧 💨 ❄ Date: M T W T F S S

What we did today:

Our favourite books today:

Today I loved...

Something I am grateful for today:

Today I felt: 😀 🙂 😊 😋 😆 😌 🤨 😟 ☹ 😠

My Epic Toddler Journal

Weather: ☀ ☁ 🌈 🌧 💨 ❄   Date: M T W T F S S

What we did today:

Our favourite books today:

What I remember about today...

Something I am grateful for today:

Today I felt: 😀 🙂 😍 😜 😆 😌 😕 😟 ☹ 😠

My Epic Toddler Journal   115

ADVENTURE
IS OUT THERE

Weather: ☀️ ☁️ 🌈 🌧️ 💨 ❄️   Date: M T W T F S S

What we did today:

Our favourite books today:

Today we did this...

Something I am grateful for today:

Today I felt: 😃 🙂 😍 😜 😆 😌 😟 😰 ☹️ 😠

My Epic Toddler Journal   117

Weather: ☀ ☁ 🌈 🌧 💨 ❄ Date: M T W T F S S

What we did today:

Our favourite books today:

I saw this today...

Something I am grateful for today:

Today I felt: 😀 🙂 😍 😋 😆 😌 😟 😖 🙁 😠

My Epic Toddler Journal

Weather: ☀ ☁ 🌈 🌧 💨 ❄   Date: M T W T F S S

What we did today:

Our favourite books today:

Today we...

Something I am grateful for today:

Today I felt: 😀 🙂 😍 😜 😆 😊 😟 😰 🙁 😠

My Epic Toddler Journal   119

WATER CYCLE - EXPERIMENT

INGREDIENTS
Water
Food colouring - blue
Ziploc Bag
Permanent Marker
Tape

METHOD

1. Draw a basic landscape on the bag with a permanent marker, either showing sea or land at the base and clouds/sunshine in the 'sky'

2. Ask your toddler to pour water into the bag, about a cupful should be enough, not enough to make it too heavy.

3. Ask your toddler, or yourself, put a couple of drops of blue food colouring into the bag. Seal the bag closed then give it a little shake.

4. Tape it to a window that gets lotsof sunshine, then try to stop them from poking it too much while the magic happens.

TIPS FOR PLAY

1. Talk through the water cycle of evaporation, the clouds storing the water and then rain.

2. Talk about what water is used for, see if they can tell you anything that uses water - bathtime, drink, flowers etc Tell them more ways and help them to see how important water is.

3. Keep coming back to the water cycle bag throughout the day and see it changing and the rain falling down the bag. When you come back to it, see if they can remember the ways water is used again.

visit myepicjournals.com for more activities

Pictures of my experiments.....

Weather: ☀ ☁ 🌈 🌧 💨 ❄ Date: M T W T F S S

What we did today:

Our favourite books today:

Today I felt...

Something I am grateful for today:

Today I felt: 😀 🙂 😍 😛 😆 😌 😕 😖 ☹ 😠

122

My Epic Toddler Journal

Weekly Check In:

This week, for the first time I...:

My favourite meals this week:

Books I've read this week:

Favourite Toys to play with this week:

My favourite thing this week:

I made someone most proud when:

Weather: ☀ ☁ 🌈 🌧 💨 ❄   Date: M T W T F S S

What we did today:

Our favourite books today:

My today...

Something I am grateful for today:

Today I felt: 😀 🙂 😍 😜 😆 😌 🤢 😟 😨 😠

My Epic Toddler Journal

out of all the kids in the whole world

how did I get the

cutest

Weather: ☀ ☁ 🌈 🌧 💨 ❄   Date: M T W T F S S

What we did today:

Our favourite books today:

Today I loved...

Something I am grateful for today:

Today I felt: 😀 🙂 😍 😛 😆 😌 😕 😟 ☹ 😠

Weather: ☀ ☁ 🌈 🌧 💨 ❄   Date: M T W T F S S

What we did today:

Our favourite books today:

What I remember about today...

Something I am grateful for today:

Today I felt: 😀 🙂 😍 😋 😆 😊 😟 😖 ☹ 😠

My Epic Toddler Journal   127

Weather: ☀️ ☁️ 🌈 🌧️ 💨 ❄️ Date: M T W T F S S

What we did today:

Our favourite books today:

Today we did this...

Something I am grateful for today:

Today I felt: 😃 🙂 😍 😜 😆 😌 😕 😖 ☹️ 😠

I can draw where I live...　　　　　Date: _____

Weather: ☀️ ☁️ 🌈 🌧️ 💨 ❄️ Date: M T W T F S S

What we did today:

Our favourite books today:

I saw this today...

Something I am grateful for today:

Today I felt: 😀 🙂 😍 😛 😆 😌 🤔 😟 ☹️ 😠

130

My Epic Toddler Journal

Weather: ☀ ☁ 🌈 🌧 💨 ❄   Date: M T W T F S S

What we did today:

Our favourite books today:

Today we...

Something I am grateful for today:

Today I felt: 😃 🙂 😍 😛 😆 😊 😟 😖 🙁 😠

Weather: ☀ ☁ 🌈 🌧 💨 ❄ Date: M T W T F S S

What we did today:

Our favourite books today:

Today I felt...

Something I am grateful for today:

Today I felt: 😀 🙂 😍 😜 😆 😌 🤢 😟 ☹ 😣

132

My Epic Toddler Journal

Stick in some favourite photo's or draw your favourite things

Weekly Check In:

This week, for the first time I...:

My favourite meals this week:

Books I've read this week:

Favourite Toys to play with this week:

My favourite thing this week:

I made someone most proud when:

Weather: ☀ ☁ 🌈 🌧 💨 ❄ Date: M T W T F S S

Our favourite books today:

My today…

Today I felt: 😀 🙂 😊 😋 😆 😌 😕 😖 ☹ 😠

My Epic Toddler Journal

135

Weather: ☀ ☁ 🌈 🌧 💨 ❄   Date: M T W T F S S

What we did today:

Our favourite books today:

Today I loved...

Something I am grateful for today:

Today I felt: 😀 🙂 😍 😜 😆 😌 🤔 😟 ☹ 😠

Weather: Date: M T W T F S S

What we did today:

Our favourite books today:

What I remember about today…

Something I am grateful for today:

Today I felt:

My Epic Toddler Journal

137

COLOUR OUR WORLD

Weather: ☀ ☁ 🌈 🌧 💨 ❄ Date: M T W T F S S

What we did today:

Our favourite books today:

Today we did this...

Something I am grateful for today:

Today I felt: 😀 🙂 😍 😛 😆 😌 🤕 😟 ☹ 😠

My Epic Toddler Journal

Weather: ☀ ☁ 🌈 🌧 💨 ❄   Date: M T W T F S S

What we did today:

Our favourite books today:

I saw this today...

Something I am grateful for today:

Today I felt: 😀 🙂 😍 😛 😆 😌 🤔 😖 🙁 😠

Weather: ☀ ☁ 🌈 🌧 💨 ❄   Date: M T W T F S S

What we did today:

Our favourite books today:

Today we...

Something I am grateful for today:

Today I felt: 😀 🙂 😍 😛 😆 😊 😟 😖 ☹ 😠

My Epic Toddler Journal   141

Me with friends

Weather: ☀️ ☁️ 🌈 🌧️ 💨 ❄️ Date: M T W T F S S

What we did today:

Our favourite books today:

Today I felt...

Something I am grateful for today:

Today I felt: 😀 🙂 😍 😜 😆 😌 🤔 😖 🙁 😠

explore the world around you

Weekly Check In:

This week, for the first time I...:

My favourite meals this week:

Books I've read this week:

Favourite Toys to play with this week:

My favourite thing this week:

I made someone most proud when:

Weather: ☀️ ☁️ 🌈 🌧️ 💨 ❄️   Date: M T W T F S S

What we did today:

Our favourite books today:

My today...

Something I am grateful for today:

Today I felt: 😀 🙂 😍 😛 😆 😌 😟 😖 😕 😠

Weather: ☀️ ☁️ 🌈 🌧️ 💨 ❄️   Date: M T W T F S S

What we did today:

Our favourite books today:

Today I loved...

Something I am grateful for today:

Today I felt: 😀 🙂 😍 😜 😆 😊 😟 😖 😕 😠

My Epic Toddler Journal   *147*

Arctic Ocean
North America
Atlantic Ocean
Europe
Asia
Pacific Ocean
Africa
South America
Pacific Ocean
Indian Ocean
Australia
Antarctica

Weather: ☀ ☁ 🌈 🌧 💨 ❄   Date: M T W T F S S

What we did today:

Our favourite books today:

What I remember about today...

Something I am grateful for today:

Today I felt: 😀 🙂 😍 😛 😆 😊 🤢 😟 🙁 😣

My Epic Toddler Journal

149

Weather: ☀ ☁ 🌈 🌧 💨 ❄ Date: M T W T F S S

What we did today:

Our favourite books today:

Today we did this...

Something I am grateful for today:

Today I felt: 😀 🙂 🥰 😋 😆 😌 🤔 😖 ☹ 😠

My Epic Toddler Journal

Weather: ☀ ☁ 🌈 🌧 💨 ❄   Date: M T W T F S S

What we did today:

Our favourite books today:

I saw this today...

Something I am grateful for today:

Today I felt: 😀 🙂 😍 😋 😆 😌 😟 😖 😣 😠

My Epic Toddler Journal   *151*

Pictures of my favourite things

Weather: ☀ ☁ 🌈 🌧 💨 ❄ Date: M T W T F S S

What we did today:

Our favourite books today:

Today we...

Something I am grateful for today:

Today I felt: 😀 🙂 😍 😜 😆 😌 😟 😣 🙁 😠

My Epic Toddler Journal 153

Weather: ☀ ☁ 🌈 🌧 💨 ❄ Date: M T W T F S S

What we did today:

Our favourite books today:

Today I felt...

Something I am grateful for today:

Today I felt: 😀 🙂 😍 😜 😆 😌 😟 😖 ☹ 😠

154

My Epic Toddler Journal

Weekly Check In:

This week, for the first time I...:

My favourite meals this week:

Books I've read this week:

Favourite Toys to play with this week:

My favourite thing this week:

I made someone most proud when:

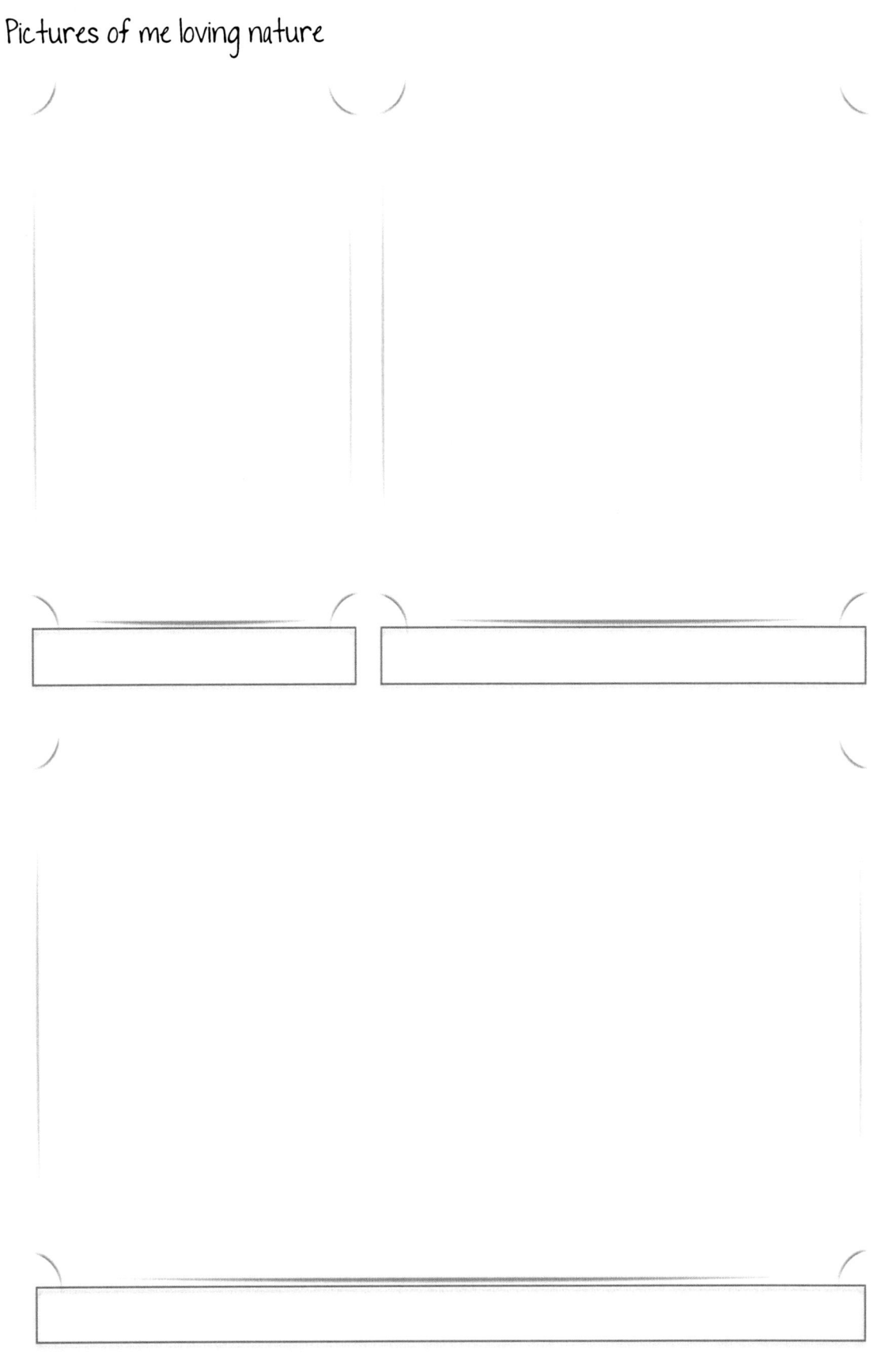

Pictures of me loving nature

Reflection Page

Use this space to write a note to your little one this month. Did you go anywhere new that they enjoyed? Did they do something to make you proud? Did they do something kind? Did they make you laugh? Maybe share how much you love them. Tell them a story, or write down a story they told you.

A note from the creator:

Thank you for choosing to use this Nurtured.me My EPIC Toddler Journal. I hope you enjoyed completing this journal each day as much as I enjoyed creating it. To carry on your journalling journey together, there are further journals in this series. To find out more, you can head to:

www.myepicjournals.com or www.nurtured.me

Rachael Cartmell x

Made in the USA
Middletown, DE
12 December 2019